ISBN: 9781764274593

First Edition

Fruitful Frilled-Neck

Conflict and Connection

Pippa Bird

Frank the Frilled-Neck Lizard was known for his
grumpy moods, although often he was known for
his kindness.

Complimented Pretzel Python's twisty dance.

He helped Piper Potoroo build her leaf nest.

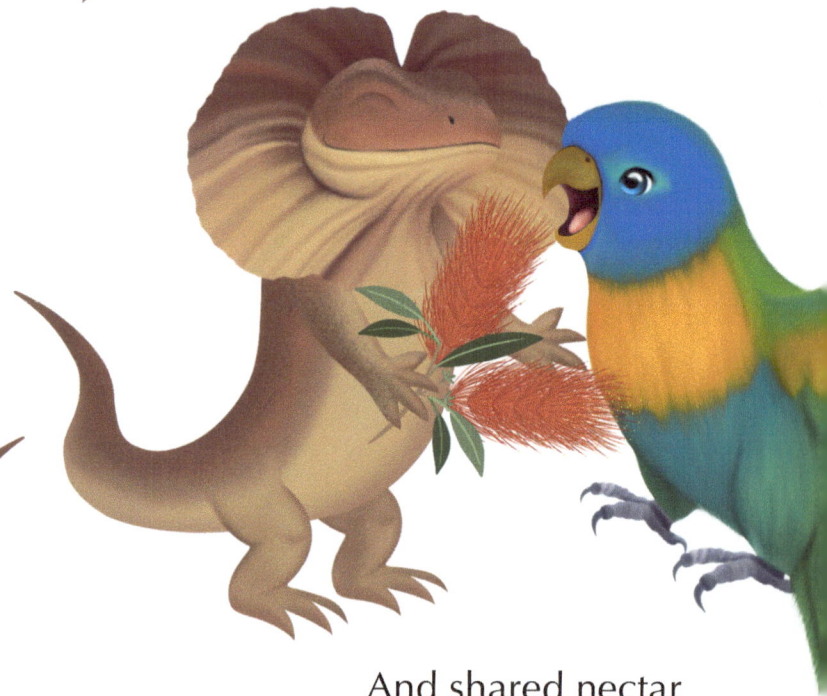

And shared nectar with Larry Lorikeet.

His frill flared with
joy when he was
helping others.

And it would often
flare when he was
frustrated.

Tallulah the Talkative Tortoise was wise and well-meaning.
She had stories tucked into every wrinkle of her shell.

But when she spoke, her words came in long, winding rivers, and she often forgot to pause. Frank tried to listen, but her stories sometimes overwhelmed him.

One morning, as Tallulah began a tale about her shell-polishing days, Frank interrupted sharply, hissing with his tongue poking out.

"Can I just finish what I was saying?"
he snapped, walking around the bush
with his arms folded.

Tallulah blinked. Felix, Frank's
young nephew, watched from afar,
intrigued by this behaviour.

Felix watched everything Frank did.
He admired his uncle's strength, his
kindness, his frill.

He wanted to be
just like him.

Later that day, Felix repeated
Frank's words to Larry Lorikeet.
"Can I just finish?" he said, his tiny
frill flaring.

Larry felt angry and hurt, flying
away. Frank overheard.

"Felix! That's rude. We don't speak like that."
Felix blinked. "But… you did."

Frank brushed it off. "I'm an adult. You're still learning."

The next day, Tallulah visited again. Frank sighed and snapped, "Not now."

Felix echoed the phrase with Pretzel Python.

Again, Frank scolded him. "You need to be polite, Felix."

Felix's frill drooped. "But I was doing as you do."

By the third day, Felix had stopped
dancing with Pretzel. He sat alone near
the billabong, holding a smooth river
stone Kirri had given him weeks ago.

Kirri noticed.

But she also noticed something else. Tallulah had wandered off into the bush, her shell scraped softly against the underbrush as she moved. Slower than usual, quieter than ever.

Kirri followed the trail of flattened grass and found Tallulah sitting beneath a hollow tree.

"You're quiet today," Kirri said gently.

Tallulah sighed. "I'm trying to be less… much. I think my talkativeness annoys others. Frank snapped. Felix flinched. I thought stories were my way of connecting. But maybe I've been too loud for too long."

Kirri tilted her head. "Your stories are gifts, Tallulah. But even gifts need wrapping - pauses…invitations…space to breathe."

Tallulah blinked. "So I shouldn't stop talking?"

"No," Kirri smiled. "But you might ask first. 'Would you like a story?' is a gentle way to offer, not overwhelm."

Tallulah nodded slowly.
"I can do that."

Kirri placed a paw on the tortoises cheek. "Your voice matters. It just needs room to land."

They sat together in silence - a new kind of story unfolding between them.

Then Kirri hopped toward the western edge of the bush,
back where she left two very frustrated frilled-necks.

She didn't announce herself. She simply observed.

Frank was pacing near the billabong, his frill twitching with frustration. Felix sat nearby, curled around his river stone, eyes downcast. The space between them was wide - not in distance, but in feeling.

Frank muttered to himself. "I'm trying. I really am."

Felix didn't respond. He was mimicking the silence now, unsure if speaking would earn praise or correction.

Kirri stayed hidden behind a large fern, watching with soft eyes. She saw the ripple - the way Frank's tone had echoed into Felix's actions, and now into his withdrawal.

She stepped forward, her presence gentle but grounding.

"Sometimes," she said, "the loudest lessons are taught in silence."

Frank's face dropped. "I didn't mean to hurt him."

"I know," Kirri replied. "But intention and impact don't always walk hand in hand."

She turned to Felix. "Would you like to speak?"

Felix nodded slowly. "I want to be like Uncle Frank. But I don't know which parts to copy."

Kirri smiled. "Then let's sort the echoes together. Come on, let's take a walk."

"Firstly, we must pause and take a deep breath. Then we must ask ourselves several questions. This will help us notice if what we say is what we mean."

"We can ask questions like, 'Did my words hurt someone's feelings? What did my heart hear?'"

"Did I say what I meant, 'I wanted to help. Did it feel kind or confusing?'"

"How can I fix the feeling that I caused? 'Let's find softer words or a gentler way. How could I say this in a nice way?'"

"And lastly, what could we do to repair the hurt we may have accidentally caused? 'We're still a team. We grow like trees - together.' And perhaps offer a hug."

"Felix, does that sound like it might help next time?" finished Kirri.

"Yes, I think I can try that," replied Felix.

Frank stood beside Felix.
"I'm still learning too," he said. "I didn't realise how loud my frill was. And I certainly didn't realise you were watching me so closely. I'm sorry."

"I'm always watching, Uncle Frank. I want to be just like you when I grow up. But sometimes I get confused."

"Then let's practice together," Frank said.

The frilled-necks embraced each other with a warm hug.

Later, Tallulah arrived
with a new story - but
this time, she asked first.
"Would you like a tale
about river stones?"

Frank looked at his nephew
and smiled. "Yes, please."
Felix beamed with excitement.

Kirri smiled and spoke softly to herself, "The clearing," she said, "is quieter now. But fuller too."

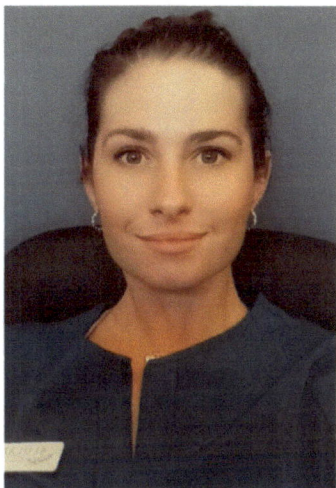

About the Author
Pippa Bird is a former Mental Health Therapist in Private Practice Alula Blu Counselling Services, in regional NSW

Pippa holds a Bachelor in Psychology, a Diploma in Counselling, and a Diploma in Graphic Design, with a primary focus on illustration.

Calm Kangaroo

CALM KANGAROO is a backronym title for a children's mental and emotional well-being program. An initiative designed to educate children about mental health and foster a learning journey of emotional intelligence, resilience and cultivate an open mind through the benefits of reading well-being books, leading to the most important discussions and ideas.

CALM KANGAROO focuses on Curating, Advocating & Leading Mindfulness, & its mission to Kindle Awareness, Nurture Growth, Amplify Resilience, & Orchestrate Open-minds.

Calm Kangaroo series by Pippa Bird. Available on Amazon.

9 781764 274593